The Finished Work of Christ

Get ready to receive all that Jesus has accomplished. Freedom in Christ awaits you on the pages you are about to read.

The Finished Work of Chirst

Copyright© 2023 Amber Twigg publishing a division of A.Twigg Ministries

All rights reserved. This book or any portion thereof may not be reproduced or used in any manner whatsoever, stored in a retrieval system, or transmitted in any form without the express written permission of the publisher.

All Scripture quotations, unless otherwise indicated, are taken from the Holy Bible, New International Version®, NIV®. Copyright ©1973, 1978, 1984, 2011 by Biblica, Inc.™ Used by permission of Zondervan. All rights reserved worldwide. "NIV" and "New International Version" are tradem
arks registered in the United States Patent and Trademark Office by Biblica, Inc.™

Printed in the United States of America

ISBN 9798852415042
Designer: AmberTwigg
www.Ambertwigg.com

Introduction

This workbook is designed to answer questions that keep people stuck in wrong thinking. It will show you the power of Christ, what he did for you and to you on the cross, and what that means for you. You will learn identity and freedom from legalistic traps that bring no fruit so that you can live out this glorious Jesus life.

Dedication

To my beloved Jesus the one that redeemed my life by giving me His.

To my Children Alex, Jacob, and Kingston you have taught me what it is to love and I'm so proud of you three. I love you with all my heart.

To my mother Julie Maness VanAlstine whose life has inspired me to live like Jesus.

To my Dad Daryl Wayne Frazee a wild one and whom there is never a dull moment.

Acknowledgements

Thank you Holy Spirit for revealing Jesus to me.

Thank you to every individual that pours out the message of the Crucified Christ and never holds back on sharing the Finished Work of Jesus Christ.

First, let me set the tone for this workbook with a brief note to the reader.

The whole Bible is written about Christ. When you read the Bible, please read it through the lens of what Christ accomplished on the cross, and every time you read about Jesus, place your life inside of him. You are in Christ and He is in you. Jesus died on the cross so that you could be free. Free from everything you were never meant to be. Free from rejection, shame, condemnation, and self-hatred. When someone accepts Jesus as Lord they are giving up their life in exchange for His. Now through baptism, they share in his death and this eradicates your old Sin nature. Christ doesn't leave you in the grave though, he resurrects you and gives you a brand new life. He gives you his very life. You are resurrected into everything Christ is and just as Christ is, so are you in the earth right now. I also would suggest that you read the following scriptures and Bible books that are mentioned.

Romans 6: Explains what happened to you when you died with Christ and how the old sinful nature is gone forever.

Romans 7: Tells you about the miserable life Paul had before he was able to rid himself of Sin nature through the death of Jesus Christ. In addition, it tells you that you are now in Union with Christ because the old you died in the grave with Christ.

Romans 8: Expounds on why there is no condemnation for those that are in Christ Jesus and life in the Holy Spirit and what that means for the born-again believer.

Read The entire book of Galatians & Colossians and look up the definitions of words in Strongs Concordance/ Lexicon.

Some helpful study tips before you get started...

- Learn how to use Strong's to look up the bible definitions.
- Use a regular dictionary to get more meaning from the words you read and define.
- Utilize Blue Letter Bible or Bible Hub for an in-depth study of God's word.
- Do your studies from a word-for-word Bible translation.
- Read different translations that bring enrichment to the original text.
- The whole Bible is about Christ, the Cross, and your life. You have to read it through the lens of what Christ Finished on the Cross to understand what that means for your life.

Volume 1
IDENTITY

Q Am I still a sinner now that I am in Christ?

Christ Crucified is your freedom

A No, you no longer have a sin nature. It is destroyed and you have a New Nature, the Christ nature in you.
Romans 6: 1-23
Galatians 2:20
Colossians 2: 11-13
2nd Corinthians 5:16
2nd Corinthians 5:17

Use this Example sheet as a guide to all your studying.

Please write out the bible verses and answer questions using the bible verse. Also, write out the definitions.

Example Sheet

Romans 6:6 For we know that our old self was crucified with him so that the body ruled by sin might be done away with, that we should no longer be slaves to sin. (NIV)

What was crucified with Christ?
Answer: Our old self was crucified.

Write out the meaning of the word using the Strong's Greek #3820. Definition of **Old**:

Not new or recent. antique, worn out

Write out the meaning of the word using the Strong's Greek #444. Definition of **Self**:

Man, human race, human being

Example Sheet

Write out the meaning of the word using the Strong's Greek #4957.

Definition of **Was Crucified With Him**:

Crucify with, together, become estranged dead to my former habit of feeling and action

Write out the meaning of the word using the Strong's Greek #266. Definition **of Sin**:

Failure, guilt, missing the mark

Write out the meaning of the word using the Strong's Greek #2673. Definition of **Might Be Rendered Inoperative**:

Sever, abolish, separate from, nullify, removed

Please write out the bible verses and answer questions using the bible verse. Also, write out the definitions.

Romans 6:18

What were you set free from?

Strong's Greek # 1659

Definition of **You Have been set FREE:**

Please write out the bible verses and answer questions using the bible verse. Also, write out the definitions.

Galatians 2:20

Who was crucified with Christ?

Can you be a little crucified?

Can you be a little dead?

Who lives in you now?

Can the old you be alive anymore?

Strong's Greek #3765

Definition of **No Longer**:

Please write out the bible verses and answer questions using the bible verse. Also, write out the definitions.

Colossians 2: 11-13

Did the Flesh get cut off of you now that you're in Christ?

Did Sin Nature get cut off of you?

Strong's Greek #4561

Definition of **Sinful Nature**:

Please write out the bible verses and answer questions using the bible verse. Also, write out the definitions.

2nd Corinthians 5:16

Christ Crucified is your freedom

Are we supposed to regard/know people/ourselves after the flesh now that they/we are in Christ?

Strong's Greek #4561
Definition of **The Flesh**:

Please write out the bible verses and answer questions using the bible verse. Also, write out the definitions.

2nd Corinthians 5:17

Now that you are in Christ are you made New?

Are you a New Creation now?

How did you become a new creation?

Strong's Greek #2537

Definition of **New**:

What has passed away?

Who has become New?

How did you become New?

Did you make yourself new or
Did God do it when you came into Christ?

Strong's Greek #2937

Definition of **Creation**:

Please write out the scriptures and use different bible translations to expound on the verse and enrich your understanding.

Romans 6:6

Romans 6:6

Romans 6:6

Please write out the scriptures and use different bible translations to expound on the verse and enrich your understanding.

Galatians 2:20

Galatians 2:20

Galatians 2:20

Please write out the scriptures and use different bible translations to expound on the verse and enrich your understanding.

Colossians 2:11

Christ Crucified is your freedom

Colossians 2:11

Colossians 2:11

Please write out the scriptures and use different bible translations to expound on the verse and enrich your understanding.

Romans 6:18

___

___

___

___

Romans 6:18

___

___

___

___

Romans 6:18

___

___

___

___

Please write out the scriptures and use different bible translations to expound on the verse and enrich your understanding.

2 Corinthians 5:16

2 Corinthians 5:16

2 Corinthians 5:16

Christ Crucified is your freedom

Please write out the scriptures and use different bible translations to expound on the verse and enrich your understanding.

2 Corinthians 5:17

Christ Crucified is your freedom

2 Corinthians 5:17

2 Corinthians 5:17

Notes & concluding thoughts explaining why you are no longer a sinner now that you are in Christ.

_____

_____
_____

_____

Christ Crucified

_____

is your freedom

_____

_____

_____

_____

_____

_____

_____

Notes & concluding thoughts explaining why you are no longer a sinner now that you are in Christ.

_____

_____

_____

_____

Christ Crucified

_____

is your freedom

_____

_____

_____

_____

_____

_____

_____

_____

Q Can a person that is living a life in the Holy Spirit also live a life in the flesh at the same time?

Christ Crucified is your freedom

A No. You can not live a life in the Holy Spirit and the flesh at the same time.
Galatians 5:16
Romans 8:13

Please write out the bible verses and answer questions using the bible verse. Also, write out the definitions.

Galatians 5:16

Life in the Spirit causes me not to gratify any desires of what?

Strong's Greek #4043

Definition of **Walk:**

Strong's Greek #5055

Definition of **You will not gratify:**

Please write out the bible verses and answer questions using the bible verse. Also, write out the definitions.

Romans 8:13

Christ Crucified is your freedom

Does living in the Spirit put to death the deeds of the sinful nature/body/flesh?

Strong's Greek #4234

Definition of **Deeds**:

Strong's Greek #4983

Definition of **Body**:

Please write out the scriptures and use different bible translations to expound on the verse and enrich your understanding.

Galatians 5:16

Christ Crucified is your freedom

Galatians 5:16

Galatians 5:16

Please write out the scriptures and use different bible translations to expound on the verse and enrich your understanding.

Romans 8:13

Christ Crucified is your freedom

Romans 8:13

Romans 8:13

Notes & concluding thoughts on the joy of living in the Spirit.

Notes & concluding thoughts on the joy of living in the Spirit.

Christ Crucified is your freedom

Q: Is my heart still deceitfully wicked now that I am made new in Christ?

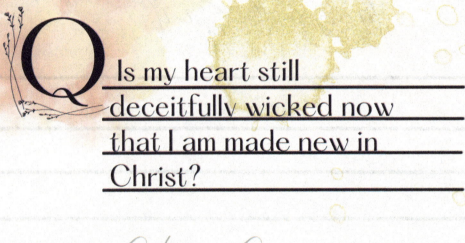
Christ Crucified is your freedom

A: No. Your heart is not wicked because you have been given a new heart when you were born again.
Jeremiah 31:33
Ezekiel 36:26
Hebrews 8:10
2nd Corinthians 5:17

Please write out the bible verses and answer questions using the bible verse. Also, write out the definitions.

Jeremiah 31:33

Ezekiel 36:26

Hebrews 8:10

2nd Corinthians 5:17

When you came into Christ did all things become New?

Do you still have an old stony heart in you now that you're born again?

Look up the word **Heart** in Ezekiel 36:26 in Strong's Hebrew #3820. Write the definition.

Look up the word **Mind** in Hebrews 8:10 in Strong's Greek #1271. Write the definition.

Please write out the scriptures and use different bible translations to expound on the verse and enrich your understanding.

Hebrews 8:10

Christ Crucified is your freedom

Hebrews 8:10

Hebrews 8:10

Notes & concluding thoughts on your new heart and mind that you have been given now that you are in Christ.

_____

_____

_____

_____

_____

_____

_____

_____

_____

_____

_____

_____

_____

_____

_____

Christ Crucified is your freedom

Notes & concluding thoughts on your new heart and mind that you have been given now that you are in Christ.

Christ Crucified is your freedom

Q Is there a difference between sin nature and the action of sin?

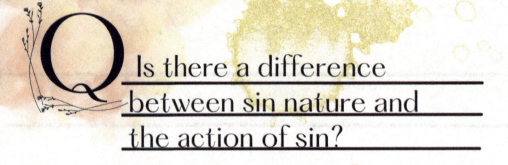
Christ Crucified is your freedom

A Yes. Sin nature is a noun it's a person, place, or thing. The action of sin is a verb. Sin nature is what got removed when you died with Jesus.
Romans 6:7

Please write out the bible verses and answer questions using the bible verse. Also, write out the definitions.

Romans 6:7

Because you died with Christ what did you get set free from?

Strong's Greek #1344

Definition of **Has Been Freed:**

The word Sin also means failure & guilt. So now that you have been set free from sin you have also been set free from failure and guilt. Now that you are set free, do you have to serve failure and guilt any longer?

Please write out the scriptures and use different bible translations to expound on the verse and enrich your understanding.

Romans 6:7

Christ Crucified is your freedom

Romans 6:7

Romans 6:7

Notes & concluding thoughts about what it means to be free from Sin, Failure, and Guilt.

Christ Crucified is your freedom

Notes & concluding thoughts about what it means to be free from Sin, Failure, and Guilt.

Christ Crucified is your freedom

Q Are you commanded to think you are dead to sin, failure, and guilt?

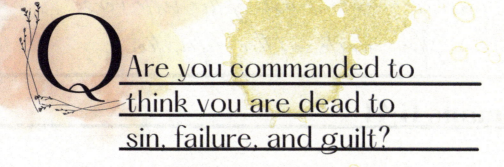
Christ Crucified is your freedom

A Yes. Absolutly You are to think/reckon/conclude/decide yourself dead to sin and alive to God.
Romans 6:11

Please write out the bible verses and answer questions using the bible verse. Also, write out the definitions.

Romans 6:11

_____

God tells you to use your mind to think you're dead to failure/sin/guilt. So should you ever refer to yourself as a failure or sinner?

Does God tell you to think of yourself by what you have done in the past or does He tell you to think about yourself without sin because the old you died with Christ?

Strong's Greek #3049

Definition of **Must Count**:

Please write out the scriptures and use different bible translations to expound on the verse and enrich your understanding.

Romans 6:11

Christ Crucified is your freedom

Romans 6:11

Romans 6:11

Notes & concluding thoughts about how i am to think of myself now that i am a New creation in Christ.

_____
_____
_____
_____
_____
_____
_____
_____
_____
_____
_____
_____
_____
_____
_____

Christ Crucified is your freedom

Notes & concluding thoughts about how I am to think of myself now that I am a New creation in Christ.

Christ Crucified is your freedom

Q Am I Holy, Blameless, Flawless, and above reproach?

Christ Crucified is your freedom

A Yes. You are because of what Christ has done for you and to you. Also, you are commanded to never let anyone persuade you any differently.
Colossians 1:22
Colossians 1:23

Please write out the bible verses and answer questions using the bible verse. Also, write out the definitions.

Colossians 1:22

Because of what Christ has done, how does God see you as you stand before Him?

Strong's Greek #40

Definition of **Holy**:

Strong's Greek #299

Definition of **Unblemished**:

Strong's Greek #410

Definition of **Blameless**:

God says you are Holy. Do you agree with Him or do you agree with your own opinion about yourself?

Jesus says you are blameless. Does God lie or is He telling the truth?

Humility accepts what Jesus says about you. Pride rejects how Jesus sees you. Are you humble or prideful?

God doesn't ask you to view yourself through the lens of your past or the mistakes you have made. Jesus tells you to look at yourself through everything He has accomplished. You are Holy, Blameless, and above reproach. How would your life change if you thought the same things that God thinks about you?

Proverbs 23:7 tells us, as a person thinks so will his or her life be. So this means your thinking dictates your perspective and how you will live out your life. Don't you think it's about time you have God's perspective for your life so that you can live the life He called you to?

What does God think about Jesus?

YOU are one with JESUS. Christ lives inside of you. Now that you know this, what does God think about YOU?

You are not your past because you died with Christ. Jesus absorbed every mistake you have ever made and will ever make. He took all of your old life before you knew Jesus and killed it on the cross with himself. Now you have the Holy One living inside of you. So what does that make you?

Please write out the bible verses and answer questions using the bible verse. Also, write out the definitions.

Colossians 1:23

What Truth must you continue to believe?

You are to establish your thinking in God's truth. Are you commanded not to drift away from this truth?

Strong's Greek #2311

Definition of **Established**:

Colossians 1:23 in the NLT version is talking about what was heard in the previous verse Colossians 1:22. These scriptures tell you that you must continue to believe this truth (that you are Holy, Blameless, and above reproach) and that you must stand in this truth and not drift away from it. Why would God tell you never to depart from this truth?

Would your thinking get healthy if you thought as Jesus does about you?

Please write out the scriptures and use different bible translations to expound on the verse and enrich your understanding.

Colossians 1:22

Colossians 1:22

Colossians 1:22

Please write out the scriptures and use different bible translations to expound on the verse and enrich your understanding.

Colossians 1:23

Christ Crucified is your freedom

Colossians 1:23

Colossians 1:23

Notes & concluding thoughts about How God sees me in His sight.

Christ Crucified is your freedom

Notes & concluding thoughts about How God sees me in His sight.

Christ Crucified is your freedom

Q Am I One Spirit with the Lord Jesus?

Christ Crucified is your freedom

A Yes. You are one with the Lord Jesus because you are joined with the Lord in his death and resurrection. You are now One with Him.
Romans 6:5
1 Corinthians 6:17

Please write out the bible verses and answer questions using the bible verse. Also, write out the definitions.

Romans 6:5

Are you united with Jesus in his death?

Are you united with Jesus in his resurrection?

Strong's Greek #4854

Definition of **United with Him:**

Please write out the bible verses and answer questions using the bible verse. Also, write out the definitions.

1 Corinthians 6:17

Are you United with the Lord?

Does one mean one?

Does this oneness in Spirit include your soul, mind, will, and emotions too?

Strong's Greek #1520

Definition of **One**:

Strong's Greek #4151

Definition of **Spirit**:

The Word for Spirit in the Strong's #4151 includes the rational spirit. The power by which a human being feels, thinks, wills, and decides; the soul. Do you know what this means now that your mind is connected to the Spirit of God?

Since we are connected to the Spirit of the Lord Jesus, we get to be transformed. However, to get transformed, we have to think differently. Because, as a person thinks, so he or she will be (Proverbs 23:7). Do you study the old unrenewed you to get transformed into the image of Christ? Or do you study Christ to upgrade your mind in the image of Christ?

This is the greatest transformation we get to partake in. God has connected us back to Himself and this allows us to renew our minds in the image of Christ. This is what brings about the transformation you have always desired. This is a victory that Christ lets us partake in. Most people get so condemned because they know they are saved but their thoughts tell them differently. You are truly made completely new. The memories of one's life are still stored in the soul/mind with its patterns of thinking before you knew Christ. Now because you are one Spirit with the Lord you get the privilege of putting in new thoughts, Christ's thoughts, so that your mind gets upgraded.

Please write out the scriptures and use different bible translations to expound on the verse and enrich your understanding.

Romans 6:5

Romans 6:5

Romans 6:5

Please write out the scriptures and use different bible translations to expound on the verse and enrich your understanding.

1 Corinthians 6:17

1 Corinthians 6:17

1 Corinthians 6:17

Christ Crucified is your freedom

Notes & concluding thoughts now that you know you are One with the Lord Jesus. Explain what this means for your life.

Christ Crucified is your freedom

Notes & concluding thoughts now that you know you are One with the Lord Jesus. Explain what this means for your life.

Christ Crucified is your freedom

Q How do you manifest the new Life in Christ?

Christ Crucified is your freedom

A You study the image of Christ and all that He is.
Colossians 3:10

Please write out the bible verses and answer questions using the bible verse. Also, write out the definitions.

Colossians 3:10

What have you put on?

Strong's Greek #1746

Definition of **Have put On**:

The word "have" is past tense. It says you have put on the new self. Why is it important to know that you already have the new self?

Is your knowledge of Christ what renews your mind and makes you think differently about yourself, your life, and Christ?

For most of our lives, we have been taught that we are our failures or the sins we have committed. However, in Christ, failure ends and you inherit a brand new life. None of your previous old life, before you knew Christ transfers over at all. You may have old mindsets and old ways of thinking but that will become less and less as you study the new man Christ Jesus. This is how you renew your mind and manifest Christ. So who do you study to manifest the Christ life?

Please write out the scriptures and use different bible translations to expound on the verse and enrich your understanding.

Colossians 3:10

Colossians 3:10

Colossians 3:10

Notes & concluding thoughts on how you are to manifest this Christ life.

Christ Crucified is your freedom

Notes & concluding thoughts on how you are to manifest this Christ life.

Christ Crucified is your freedom

Q Am I lying if I say that I am still a Sinner or failure now that I am born again?

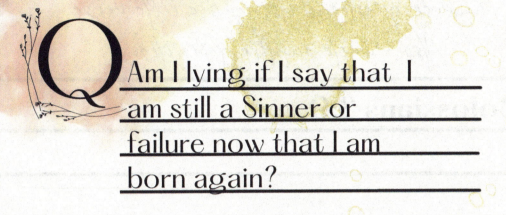
Christ Crucified is your freedom

A Yes. You are lying because the old sinful you, the old failed you, doesn't exist anymore now that you are in Christ Jesus.
Colossians 3:9

Please write out the bible verses and answer questions using the bible verse. Also, write out the definitions.

Colossians 3:9

_____
_____
_____
_____

Don't lie to who?

_____
_____

What have you put off when you came into Christ?

_____
_____

Since the old self is put off with all of its practices does this mean it's still on you?

_____
_____

Please write out the definitions.

Strong's Greek #5574

Definition of **Lie**:

Strong's Greek #554

Definition of **Since you have taken off**:

Strong's Greek #4234

Definition of **Practices**:

Please write out the scriptures and use different bible translations to expound on the verse and enrich your understanding.

Colossians 3:9

_____
_____
_____
_____
_____
_____

Colossians 3:9

_____
_____
_____
_____
_____
_____

Colossians 3:9

_____
_____
_____
_____
_____
_____

Christ Crucified is your freedom

Notes & concluding thoughts on how you are to refer to yourself now that you are made completely new.

Christ Crucified is your freedom

Notes & concluding thoughts on how you are to refer to yourself now that you are made completely new.

*Christ Crucified
is your freedom*

Q Am I just like Jesus?

Christ Crucified is your freedom

A Yes. You are just like Jesus. You don't have to wait to go to heaven to be like Christ. You are like Him now.
1 John 4:17

Please write out the bible verses and answer questions using the bible verse. Also, write out the definitions.

1 John 4:17

Why do you have confidence on the day of judgment?

Who are you like in this world?

Does it say you are a little like Jesus or that you are like Him?

Please write out the bible verses and answer questions using the bible verse. Also, write out the definitions.

Does it say you are Just like Jesus in the world or does it say you have to wait to go to heaven to be like him?

Christ Crucified is your freedom

Strong's Greek #2192

Definition of **We may have**:

Strong's Greek #3954

Definition of **Confidence**:

Strong's Greek #2889

Definition of **World**:

Please write out the definitions.

Strong's Greek #1473

Definition of **We**:

Strong's Greek #1510

Definition of **Are**:

Strong's Greek #2531

Definition of **Just like**:

Please write out the scriptures and use different bible translations to expound on the verse and enrich your understanding.

1 John 4:17

1 John 4:17

1 John 4:17

Christ Crucified is your freedom

Notes & concluding thoughts now that you know you are Just like Jesus in this world.

_____

_____

_____

_____

Christ Crucified

_____

is your freedom

_____

_____

_____

_____

_____

_____

_____

Notes & concluding thoughts now that you know you are Just like Jesus in this world.

Christ Crucified is your freedom

Congratulations on completing this workbook. Please share the revelation of your freedom in Christ with everyone you come in contact with. Keep going over this study workbook and constantly let the finished work of Christ refresh you. You will find as you continue to stay in the message of Christ it becomes richer and richer within you.

Thank you for journeying through this workbook with an open heart to know Jesus and what He accomplished for you. I pray that Christ and Him crucified becomes the only thing you know and that the new Christ-life would manifest in you fully. Bless you, greatly.

With Love,
Amber Twigg

Amber Twigg Ministries

Made in the USA
Columbia, SC
09 February 2025